War

A Primer for Christians

Joseph L. Allen

Abingdon Press
Nashville

WAR: A PRIMER FOR CHRISTIANS

Copyright © 1991 by Abingdon Press

This book is printed on recycled, acid-free paper.

Scripture quotations unless otherwise noted are from the New Revised Standard Version Bible, copyright © 1989, by the Division of Christian Education of the National Council of the Churches of Christ in the U.S.A.

Library of Congress Cataloging-in-Publication Data

Allen, Joseph L., 1928-
    War : a primer for Christians / Joseph L. Allen.
      p. cm.
    ISBN 0-687-44012-2 (pbk. : alk. paper)
    1. War—Religious aspects—Christianity.   I. Title.
BT736.2.A44   1991
241'.6242—dc20

91-14246
CIP

MANUFACTURED IN THE UNITED STATES OF AMERICA

CONTENTS

To Bob and Joyce,
their generation,
and generations yet to come.

PREFACE

When our country is not at war, few of us think through carefully what would be an adequate response to war from the standpoint of our faith. We put our minds to more immediate matters. The crisis in the Persian Gulf, in its sudden onset on August 2, 1990, and as it eventually led to actual war on January 16, 1991, reminded us of how fraught with conflict the international scene is and how quickly a war can arise. The Persian Gulf War made many people, Christians as well as others, aware of the need for an adequate way to think about war—any war—in terms of their faith.

Various resources are already available to help Christians think about war. The Bible speaks about this subject at many points, directly and indirectly, and yet this speaking lends itself to sharply conflicting interpretations. Church bodies have often made pronouncements on war, both in the distant and the more recent past, but the reasons for their judgments have not always been clear, their positions have on occasion been insufficiently self-critical, and their guidance has not always been fully consistent or sufficiently informed about the circumstances they were addressing. Moral theologians have long given serious attention to the moral issues of war, and yet their work partakes of the same shortcomings and is not easily accessible to those who are not also specialists in theology.

In addition to the above resources, a basic introduction is needed that (1) explains in a nontechnical fashion the main approaches that Christians have taken toward war and (2) examines each one critically. These are the aims of this book. Because conscientious Christians have responded to war in different and conflicting ways, it is not possible to present one framework that they all can affirm. Some Christians have supported their country's wars as crusades of good against evil; some, as pacifists, have rejected participation in or support for any war; and some have followed the just-war tradition in making discriminating moral judgments about wars. Some or all of these responses may be evident in the views of other religions and of those who affirm no religion. This book will discuss each of these three approaches in turn. About each of the three, I shall consider (1) some ways it has found expression in the Christian tradition, (2) the convictions out of which it arises and the logic with which it relates these convictions to war, and (3) its strengths and weaknesses, advantages and dangers. A concluding chapter will consider actions we might take to implement our views.

As one would expect, I have my own preference among the approaches. As a high school and college student, especially under the influence of some fellow Methodists, I was a pacifist. The writings of several theologians led me to change my mind. I came to believe that I could better express through a just-war approach the same basic convictions that had earlier led me to be a pacifist. Since then I have continued to interpret and respond to war from the standpoint of the just-war tradition.

The purpose of this book, however, is not to persuade readers to agree with my point of view. Rather I hope to present each approach as calmly and fairly as possible, so that whichever one employs, one will think more carefully and self-critically about it. One would hope that conscientious Christians would always be open to any new insight they can gain into an issue, and that even when they disagree, they would be able to discuss serious issues together. The central objective here is to encourage thoughtful reflection and response and capacity for open discussion by Christians of all convictions about the troubling and persistent problem of war.

CHAPTER ONE

Is War a Crusade?

Some Expressions of a Crusade Approach

One finds in the Old Testament a number of passages that present war between the children of Israel and their enemies as a crusade, a conflict between the forces of good and the forces of evil. Among the oldest is the story of Deborah the prophetess, judge of Israel, who strengthened the will of Barak against Sisera and the army of Canaan (Judges 4–5). Deborah did not purport to offer merely her own advice. Rather, she said, "The Lord, the God of Israel, commands you" to fight against Sisera's army; and the God of Israel assured them, "I will give him into your hand" (4:6-7). Thereafter, we are told, the oppressing Canaanites were thoroughly defeated, and the escaping Sisera was deceived and slain by Jael, a woman of Israel. Then follows "the song of Deborah," in which she exults over the victory that the Lord, the God of Israel has given the people. One finds here no hint of moral ambiguity, regret, or dismay, but unalloyed jubilation. The song concludes, "So perish all your enemies, O Lord!" (5:31).

A similar outlook is present in many other passages. Later writers, telling of the entry of the children of Israel into the promised land, declared that the Lord their God was giving them the land. Because the Lord "clears away many nations" residing there, the Israelites "must utterly destroy them. Make no covenant with them and show them no mercy" (Deut. 7:1-2). Again we are told that Joshua followed the command of the Lord and "slaughtered all the inhabitants of Ai" (Josh. 8:24), as he had those of Jericho (6:21), and as he would later do to Hazor (11:11). So also the writers portray the attitude of Samuel and Saul and David toward the Philistines and the Amalekites (cf., e.g., I Sam. 14:36, 15:1-3, II Sam. 5:22-25); of Elijah toward the prophets of Baal (I Kings 18); and, in the Apocrypha, of the Maccabees toward those who would sacrifice to heathen gods.

Since biblical times, religious and secular leaders have sometimes called for crusades. Thus Pope Urban II in 1095 called Christians to liberate the Holy Land from Moslems, whom he called wicked, accursed, and alienated from God.[1] In the wars of religion that followed the Reformation, Catholic fought against Protestant, Protestant against Catholic, and often Protestant against Anabaptist Protestant, all in the name of God and often without moral restraint. In the past two centuries we have seen the emergence of ideas of total war, which is much like the crusade in its absolute ends and lack of moral restraint. Christians and others have fought in the name of religious and nonreligious causes that they deemed absolute against what they saw as forces of evil: extremists of the French revolution against anything that smacked of the old order, communists against the forces of "reaction," Nazis and Fascists against any who resisted them, Allies against Nazis and Fascists as embodiments of all evil, Iranians against the United States as "the Great Satan," Iraqis against the evil Americans, and Western leaders against Saddam Hussein as "a new Hitler." Crusade thinking has a long history, one not confined to Christians but often present among them. In its many expressions there are certain common features, to which we shall now turn.

The Convictions and Logic of the Crusade

In the Christian tradition, there is agreement between a crusade approach and just-war teaching in certain limited respects. In both, it can sometimes be justifiable to resort to war. Further, both believe that in a particular case resort to war may be an obligation before God: that is, both approach the issue of war, like all moral questions, as a matter of religious and not merely secular morality. Beyond those points, however, the two diverge so sharply as to constitute virtually opposite ways of thinking about war.[2]

A crusade approach characteristically has these features:

1. *Crusaders see a justifiable war as a conflict between forces of good and forces of evil.* It is not merely that justice is somewhat greater on one side than on the other, as a just-war thinker would hold. For crusaders the moral distinction is absolute and unambiguous: true believers against infidels, righteous people against the unrighteous. As crusaders see it, God calls them to war, and God is actively on their side, bringing victory to the forces of righteousness. The crusaders' war is God's war, and they are God's warriors. Further, crusaders apply the absolute good/evil distinction, not simply to enemy military forces, but to whole peoples. As Edward LeRoy Long, Jr., has put it, crusaders reject not only evil deeds that the enemy *does*, but also who the enemy *is*.[3] From a crusade viewpoint, matters of degree in war are morally irrelevant.

It is easy to find this feature in Old Testament accounts of wars, as in the story of Deborah and the account of Joshua's wars against the Canaanites. Similarly in our age, this was the attitude of Nazis toward their enemies in the Second World War. In a less thoroughgoing way it was also that of some Allied leaders toward the Axis powers. An Allied air commander is reported to have justified indiscriminate bombing raids over German cities with the comment, "They were Germans!"[4] In correspondence with Winston Churchill, President Roosevelt referred to one Axis leader as "the Head Devil."[5] In the Persian Gulf War, a presumption about absolute good and evil was present in the pronouncements of President Saddam Hussein, as when he described his adversaries as forces of evil and portrayed the war as one of Moslem faith against infidels. Although President Bush's language about the war was not always that of a crusade, it did sometimes evoke that spirit, as when he described the Iraqi president as another Hitler. Whatever his intention, such a term tends to encourage people to think one side simply good and the other simply evil, and to disregard matters of degree. On the other hand, he said repeatedly that the war was not with the Iraqi people but with their leaders—a comment that tends to undermine a crusade spirit.

2. *Crusaders characteristically pursue absolute and unlimited goals.* Theirs are wars for righteousness, for the kingdom of God, for the world as they think it ought ideally to be, rather than a world in which serious evils will continue to occur. In the sixteenth and seventeenth centuries Catholics and Protestants each fought the other to advance the true faith and to eliminate heretics. Woodrow Wilson saw the First World War as a war "to make the world safe for democracy." In the Second World War, Franklin Roosevelt thought the Axis powers so evil that he rejected any negotiation with them; thus the central war aim became "unconditional surrender." The goals of the Persian Gulf War were not altogether clear. Depending on the speaker, they may have included Iraqi withdrawal from Kuwait, payment of reparations for the destruction in Kuwait, destruction of Iraq's capacity to make nuclear weapons, and/or removal of President Hussein from office. Both before and after the fighting began, some observers warned against adopting a crusade objective of utterly destroying Iraq as a military power. They pointed out that other middle eastern powers would simply move into the vacuum, and serious problems would continue in the region.

In a crusade spirit the goal of war becomes an undefined "victory"—utter and unqualified destruction of the enemy military forces and often of the enemy's government and even whole society—rather than specific limited goals in the interests of one's own side. When the ancient Romans finally defeated Carthage, they razed the city to the ground and spread salt over the ground, so that Carthage could never again exist. A "Carthagenian peace" is the ultimate in crusaders' unlimited goals. In their view, if their "Carthagenian" enemies are so unqualifiedly evil, why should they even be allowed to exist?

3. *When warfare is seen as the struggle of forces of good against evil for unlimited, absolute goals, the means of war are unrestrained.* In ancient Israel, Joshua's fighting men not only defeated the soldiers of Ai, but also slaughtered all its inhabitants (Joshua 8). The closest parallel to this in our time was the Nazis' systematic extermination of millions of Jews in the Holocaust. On a far smaller scale, the intentional bombing of noncombatants expresses a crusade approach's rejection of limited means: of those in Chinese cities by the Japanese, beginning in 1937; of Rotterdam, London, and other Allied cities by Hitler's air forces in 1940 and after; and of German and Japanese cities by the Allies from 1942 to 1945.

The case of Dresden was characteristic. For three days and nights in February, 1945, British and United States bombers attacked that German city of half a million, swollen by streams of refugees and by troops on the move. With Russian troops approaching at a distance in the east, Dresden was a strategic rail center on the river Elbe. When that bombing ended, however, the main military targets had not been significantly affected. The railroad bridges over the Elbe were still standing, and the rail yards were back in service in a few days. Yet the Allies' fire bombs (not the weapon of choice if the targets are bridges or rail yards) had killed an estimated 135,000 people, mostly civilians. In such a fashion both sides acted on the belief that in war it is morally acceptable to attack noncombatants intentionally. The very concept of noncombatants was discarded. Both sides saw the war as one in which civilians were at best pawns in the struggle, at worst willing supporters of evil. Crusaders believe that they have no moral responsibility for those who, whether in uniform or not, willingly support the evil against the good.

After General Douglas MacArthur was removed from his military command in Korea in 1951, he vividly expressed before Congress a crusader's objection to limits in war: "I am," he said, "just one hundred per cent a believer against war." But once war did begin, he said, we should fight it all-out. He thought it wrong to follow "the concept that when you use force, you can limit that force."[6]

4. *In the twentieth century a crusade approach tends to promote total war.* This is war as an unlimited effort in which all the resources of one side, human and nonhuman, are mobilized and directed against the total society of the enemy.[7] Total war mobilizes the whole society. It diverts resources from ordinary peacetime activities toward the war effort as far as possible, and it brings masses of people into the armed forces. Total war is directed against the whole social fabric. It targets not only the military, but also the essential services and ordinary peacetime activities of the enemy society, such as the distribution of food, water, and electricity. In doing this, total war exceeds the bounds of what is necessary to defeat the enemy military force and makes war on entire peoples.

Total war is enormously costly in lives and resources, both to those who are attacked and to attackers as well. It pulverizes the society of those it attacks—people, buildings, services, and the very social fabric. But it also wreaks great damage upon the attackers. It requires them to give priority to the war over all other pursuits; it drains their resources at a rapid pace; and it dislocates the ordinary fabric of social life, as through inflation, reassignment of workers to other jobs and locales, and the separation and breakup of families. People cannot be led to support total war unless they believe that the very foundations of their society are threatened. Sometimes war is this kind of threat and sometimes not. When it is, or when it is portrayed that way, people are more likely to support a crusade outlook in which the good are at war against the evil.

Leaders sometimes intentionally encourage crusade attitudes on the part of the public. They can do so by propaganda that pictures citizens of the other country as all alike, as morally depraved, as equally responsible for their government's injustices, even as all deserving death. To the extent that the public accepts this picture, it is more inclined to accept unlimited goals and unrestrained means.

Strengths and Weaknesses of a Crusade Approach

An important strength of a crusade approach is its conviction that *the causes for which countries consider going to war are morally and religiously significant.* The crises among nations always raise issues involving morality, issues about what nations and their citizens owe one another as fellow inhabitants of the world. International conflict is never rightly separable from moral examination. Furthermore, Christians understand all practical moral problems as also matters of religion. That is both because God is the ultimate source and pattern of moral action, and because in war as well as in other contexts all should be obedient to God. This is an insight recognized alike by pacifists and in the just-war tradition. It is a truth that, as we shall see, needs to be incorporated into a more adequate religious and moral perspective. The problem with a crusade approach is not that it interprets war religiously, but in the kind of religious interpretation it offers. Its interpretation involves four serious problems.

1. The most fundamental problem of a crusade is a religious one. *Its views imply an inadequate understanding of God.* Crusaders talk as though God does not care for our enemies, but only for our own side, and as though God does not lament the loss of enemy lives. That is indeed the outlook expressed in some Old Testament passages, as in Deborah's "So perish all your enemies, O Lord!" and when the Book of Deuteronomy has the Lord command, "Make no covenant to them and show them no mercy" (7:2). Because they believe that God does not value the enemy, crusaders' reaction to the killing of the enemy is one of rejoicing.

This crusading view of God conflicts sharply with other biblical passages. There is, for instance, the Old Testament portrayal of God who sends Jonah to prophesy even to the wicked city of

Nineveh (cf. also Gen. 1:27, 9:8-10, and Amos 9:7). It is also incompatible with Jesus' most telling test of what it means to love: "But I say to you, Love your enemies and pray for those who persecute you, so that you may be children of your Father in heaven; for he makes his sun rise on the evil and on the good, and sends rain on the righteous and on the unrighteous" (Matt. 5:44-45; cf. Luke 6:27, John 3:16, and Rom. 12:17-21). From a Christian standpoint all are in covenant together, whether they know it or not, act like it or not, because God has created them all to live together in peace and justice as fellow creatures.

2. The second serious problem of a crusade approach is that *it is morally simplistic.* It converts every matter of degree in morality into a simple either/or—into a conflict between the good and the evil. That outlook encourages self-righteousness on the part of the crusader, who always assumes that he or she is on the good side. Such a simple view is false to our own experience, for when we examine ourselves we know that given enough temptation, or given a deep enough crisis, we might do things as bad as what we condemn in others. "There but for the grace of God go I." As it is, we are more involved in moral evils than we want to admit. Dividing people into the good and the evil contradicts the Christian conviction that, as Paul puts it, "all have sinned and fall short of the glory of God" (Rom. 3:23). Because sin is universal, all persons are mixtures of good and evil. Assigning them neatly to the one category or the other ignores the way life is.

3. *Crusaders' absolute goals seem to presume that a crusade might bring about perfect conditions in the world.* They think a crusade might get rid of dangerous conflict for all time, or might eradicate evil people. When people seek unlimited instead of limited goals, they often bring about evils as bad as those they were fighting. War for ideal conditions can encourage destruction far beyond what is needed to restrain other countries' unjust actions. Thus by seeking "unconditional surrender" of Germany, the Allies put aside restraints and destroyed far more lives than

they might have. At the same time they helped enhance the power of the Stalinist Soviet Union. 4. Finally, *a crusade approach is indiscriminate about the enemy people.* Lumping all citizens of the enemy country together as evil implies that enemy citizens are accountable for many things that they could not have prevented. It wrongly implies that what the ordinary citizen is doing, by going about the usual details of life, is the same thing morally as what enemy troops are doing when they promote or protect an unjust regime. The crusader lacks compassion for the victims of war when those victims are on the other side. Yet once the war is over, people often discover how much like themselves the citizens of an enemy country are. It is better to realize that from the start.

In sum, for all the moral and religious earnestness of crusaders, it is difficult to see how some of their most basic views toward war can be squared with Christian belief and with ordinary human experience. Many Christians have been crusaders, at least at one time or another. If that outlook is insufficient, it is important not to adopt a similar crusading stance by rejecting crusaders as persons. From a Christian viewpoint, we are called to affirm those who differ with us, at the same time that we express our differences.

CHAPTER TWO

The Pacifist Standpoint

Pacifism in the Christian Tradition

Prior to 312 C.E.* no Christian writer approved of Christians' going to war, and very few Christians served in the military. There were several reasons for this, including expectation of the early end of this world, reluctance to join the army of their persecutors, and the danger that in the Roman army, Christians might be asked to commit idolatry—to sacrifice to the emperor or at least to approve of doing so.

A more enduring reason was the belief that killing was simply incompatible with Jesus' love command. Christian pacifists early and late have pointed to Jesus' commands not to resist evil (Matt. 5:39) and to "Love your enemies and pray for those who persecute you" (5:44; cf. Luke 6:27ff., 35). They have seen in the refusal to resist evil the expression of *agape* love as Jesus taught and exemplified it. Love is a spirit that does not seek its own good but the good of the neighbor (I Cor. 10:24), that seeks to "overcome evil with good" rather than to return evil for evil (Rom. 12:17, 21), that is sacrificial even to the point of giving up one's life (cf. Matt. 16:24-25; Mk. 8:34-35; Luke 9:23-24). From this understanding of love, pacifists have usually interpreted the sixth commandment of the law to mean "You shall not kill" (RSV, Exod. 20:13; Deut. 5:17), ruling out any taking of human life, rather than the equally plausible and less restrictive translation, "You shall not commit murder" (NEB, cf. NRSV).

---

*The Common Era, sometimes signified by A.D.

Pacifists have pointed to various Old Testament passages that are compatible with their rejection of all killing. First, there are prophetic passages that warn the people against relying upon force against their enemies (e.g., Hos. 7:11; Isa. 30:15-16). Pacifists have sometimes interpreted these passages as universal prohibitions against using force, though they can also be read simply as counsel for specific situations.

Second, there are visions of a world of peace, such as "They shall beat their swords into plowshares, and their spears into pruning hooks; nation shall not lift up sword against nation, neither shall they learn war any more" (Isa. 2:4; cf. Mic. 4:3-4; see also Isa. 9:4-6; 11:6-9; and Ps. 85:8-10). Pacifists and nonpacifists alike have understood such passages to be expressions of hope in God, but they have differed over how to interpret them. Some pacifists have seen in the prophets' visions a picture of this world as it might sometime come to be. Other pacifists and many nonpacifists have interpreted them as judgment upon the world's violence and an ideal that people should keep before them in a world of conflict.

Ordinarily, though, Christian pacifists have based their rejection of all war primarily on their interpretation of Jesus' teaching and example of love. They have appealed especially to his commands, "Do not resist an evildoer. But if anyone strikes you on the right cheek, turn the other also" (Matt. 5:39), and "Love your enemies and pray for those who persecute you" (Matt. 5:44).

After 312 C.E. and the end of Roman persecution of Christians, many Christians began to see the empire's maintenance of order and its restraint of injustice in a different light. They came to believe that it was important both to resist criminals within and to restrain the hordes of barbarians on the frontier who threatened to destroy western civilization. During the century that followed, Ambrose and Augustine developed the first outlines of Christian just-war teaching, arguing that under some circumstances it can be justifiable to go to war. Of that we shall say more in the following chapter. One result of this development, however, was that pacifism ceased to be the prevailing position within Christianity. Yet Christian pacifism has persisted throughout the church's history. In the fourth century, the theologians who believed that some wars could be justifiable for the laity also taught that the clergy could not go to war. Their nonviolence was considered a higher way. A similar belief was present in the monastic movement. In the Middle Ages there were pacifist tendencies among the Franciscans. Other groups, like the Waldensians, the Cathari, and one branch of Hussites, were pacifist. During the Reformation and afterward there arose several peace churches—Mennonites and Hutterites, and during the seventeenth and eighteenth centuries, the Quakers and Brethren.[1] In the twentieth century, in addition to the peace churches, strong pacifist movements have arisen within other Protestant denominations and among Catholics. Thus pacifism has persisted in all periods of Christian history. Over the years there have been certain enduring features of Christian pacifists' thinking about war, to which we shall now turn.

The Convictions and Logic of Pacifism

A pacifist is one who believes that it is always wrong to go to war. Ordinarily pacifists also reject other uses of violence (understanding violence here in the sense of inflicting physical or psychological injury). We shall, however, restrict our attention to their views toward war.

One is not a pacifist simply because one works for peace or values it highly. Nonpacifists also value peace highly, whether peace is taken to mean (1) the absence of war or (2) the presence of justice and concord within a community. Nonpacifists usually believe, though, that under some circumstances peace (in either sense) is possible only after forces threatening or attacking others have been violently restrained. Pacifists and nonpacifists alike can and do work for peace, but they often differ over what constitutes effective peacemaking. I shall discuss this idea further in chapter 4.

It is important to note that pacifists believe that war is *always* wrong. One is not a pacifist simply because one believes that this war or that is unjustifiable, or that most wars are unjustifiable, or even that it is unlikely that there could be a justifiable war today. Just-war thinkers could come to any of those conclusions, since they believe that using the just-war criteria might lead one either to approve or disapprove morally of a particular war. In contrast, a pacifist, as the term is generally used, does not recognize any conditions under which it would ever be right to go to war.

For this reason the terms "nuclear pacifist" or "selective pacifist" can be misleading. The term "nuclear pacifist" refers to someone who opposes any use of nuclear weapons or perhaps any war that would have a serious risk of escalating to nuclear war. Those who hold this view may use just-war criteria to support their judgments, as when they judge that nuclear weapons would always cause disproportionately great harm. Because they might support some other kinds of wars, they are not pacifists in the sense discussed here. The term "selective pacifist" confuses the issues between true pacifists and just-war thinkers. Presumably a "selective pacifist" is one who believes that some wars (however few) might be justifiable and others unjustifiable. But that is exactly what supporters of just-war teaching believe.

One must then be either a pacifist or a nonpacifist; there are no mixtures or middle possibilities. Either all wars everywhere under all conditions are wrong, as pacifists hold, or some wars might be justifiable, as just-war thinkers hold. There is a good reason for using the term "pacifist" this way. The argument that some wars might be justifiable presupposes some different beliefs and makes use of different criteria from the argument that no war could ever be justifiable, as we shall see.

Christian pacifists and just-war thinkers do, however, hold some basic theological beliefs in common. One shared belief of special significance for war is that all people are of worth in

God's sight and that therefore we ought to recognize that worth, among enemies as well as allies. On this they contrast sharply with crusaders' absolute distinction between good and evil and rejection of all enemy people as forces of evil. Shared regard for the worth of all means that there is a sense in which the disagreements between pacifists and just-war thinkers, however deep and enduring, are "within the family." This is far less the case in the relation of both positions to crusade ethics.

A fundamental issue between Christian pacifists and just-war thinkers is whether war can ever be an expression of Christian love. For pacifists it seems incredible that one might affirm *agape* love for another person and yet put that person to death. It seems equally incredible to just-war thinkers that one would be unwilling ever to go to war to protect the weak and the oppressed when no other means would effectively protect them.

There are two main types of arguments that are used to support Christian pacifists' position of opposition to all wars. The first is often referred to as the "pragmatic" argument, and the second, as the "witnessing" argument.

The pragmatic argument for pacifism. This argument asserts that a nonviolent method "works"—it resists wrongdoing in the world in a much more effective way and at less cost in human life than does war. Richard Gregg speaks of nonviolence as "moral jiu-jitsu," because it throws the other person off balance who was preparing to use violence. "The victim not only lets the attacker come, but, as it were, pulls him forward by kindness, generosity and voluntary suffering, so that the attacker loses his moral balance." He points to the nonviolent campaign of Mohandas Gandhi for Indian independence and to that of Dr. Martin Luther King, Jr., as in the Montgomery bus boycott of 1955–56, as good examples of "the power of nonviolence." In Gregg's opinion nonviolent people do have superior power: they have the moral initiative, their methods are unexpected by their violent adversaries, and they act from a spirit of calmness and self-control. Because users of nonviolence do not seek to injure or humiliate their opponents or to crush their wills, their actions can evoke a better response from their attackers and can lead to reconciliation. Furthermore, says Gregg, the same is true of international relations; nonviolence would be "an effective substitute for war."[2]

Pacifists who focus upon this argument do not usually say much about their theoretical ethical principles. Yet a principle that appears to underlie this argument is that we ought to act in a way that will bring about the best overall consequences in the world—the utilitarian principle. The pragmatic argument is that nonviolence is morally preferable to war because it produces better consequences. A pragmatic pacifist is one who claims that nonviolence *always* brings better results than war.

The witnessing argument for pacifism. Many Christian pacifists, including some who also offer the pragmatic argument, put the weight of their pacifism upon the second, "witnessing," argument. They argue that whether nonviolence produces better consequences or not, war is always wrong for a more basic reason: it is incompatible with a Christian understanding of God—incompatible with what it means to be a follower of Jesus. The Christian witness to Christ must, they say, always reject war.

John Howard Yoder,[3] a Mennonite, puts the pragmatic argument aside. It may sometimes be true that nonviolence will bring a better outcome than violence, he says, but one cannot always show that to be true. But the issue for Yoder is not whether we can control history, either violently or nonviolently; rather it is whether our action reflects God's character and obeys the call of Christ to discipleship. God's character is love, and Christians are to love as God does—without limits and without conditions. Christ accepted the role of suffering servant without violence and without complaint, and to be his disciple means to do likewise.

Yoder does not call for Christians to withdraw from the world of political life. Nor does he reject all use of power; it is ultimately God's power and therefore good. Rather, Christians must refuse to use power violently, and they must refuse to collaborate with political structures that in their violence are rebellious against God. They must refuse "to use unworthy means even for what seems to be a worthy end."[4] At the same time, Yoder recognizes a certain legitimacy on the part of a just state, even when it uses violence to restrain evil-doing. He writes of two "aeons" that coexist in our history—an aeon of sin, centered around human beings, and an aeon of redemption, centered around Christ. In the midst of an aeon of sin, God allows the state a limited police function, even to the point of using a minimum of violence. But Christians, representing the aeon of redemption, are not called to use violence; they are not even to be police.[5]

From Yoder's point of view, then, Christians are called to be obedient to Christ, not to calculate what will be effective in the world of powers. The refusal to use violence may even result in more deaths and more destruction; Yoder appears to recognize that as a possibility. Even if that is the outcome, Christians are not to participate in war and other forms of violence. It is, after all, not their action that will bring about the Kingdom; God will bring the Kingdom by God's own action at the time of God's choosing.

Stanley Hauerwas,[6] a United Methodist, offers a witnessing argument for pacifism that is similar to Yoder's. Christians find their true identity, he writes, in the church's narrative about Jesus, which at the same time is a narrative about what God is like. In Hauerwas's interpretation, Jesus rejects the dominion which is based on forcing others to do his will; he rejects any kind of violence or coercion. In like fashion, the church is not to use society's violent and coercive means; it is not to use or support violence to bring about some social good—not even to bring a greater justice. The church is called to witness to Christ, to embody Jesus' life of the cross in its own life, and in so doing to show society what it should truly be like.

The relation of Hauerwas's witnessing argument to the pragmatic argument is not fully clear. It is not that he offers an argument that nonviolence will work better than violence. The unclarity arises from his belief that society can get along for the most part without violence. Hauerwas writes, "Most governmental functions, even within the military, do not depend on coercion and violence."[7] He seems less convinced than Yoder that violence is essential to the state's role in maintaining a relatively just order. Sometimes pacifists offer both the pragmatic and the witnessing arguments for their positions. Martin Luther King, Jr., may have done that. He certainly believed that the rejection of all violence, including war, was an essential part of the meaning of love. He also believed that, at least in many situations, a method of nonviolent resistance could be an effective way to oppose injustice—much more effective than resorting to violence. Perhaps he believed that nonviolence could always be more effective.[8]

Strengths and Weaknesses of Christian Pacifism

Even though some pacifists offer both arguments for their position, the two arguments are readily distinguishable. Because they depend upon different kinds of reasons, it is best to evaluate them separately. The pragmatic argument rests mainly on a picture of how power is exercised in the world, both among individuals and among large groups like nation states. It relies upon the expectation that people and nation-states will respond to nonviolence nonviolently. Assessing the pragmatic argument therefore calls for an appraisal of its picture of how individuals and groups behave in struggles for power. The witnessing argument, on the other hand, rests on a very different kind of basis—a theological argument about the character of God and what it means to be a disciple of Christ, including a judgment about the meaning of love. To assess this argument we must focus upon its theological beliefs.

1. *Values and limits of the pragmatic argument*

The pragmatic argument identifies some significant insights into human conflicts. First, *it recognizes a wide array of effective methods of political action.* Those who wish to protest injustice, especially within relatively democratic countries, are not left only with violent options. They can advance their cause with knowledge of the psychology and methods of nonviolence.[9]

Second, *in many circumstances nonviolent means can be more effective than violence in promoting a group's goals.* King's campaign for racial justice in the United States was especially on behalf of a minority of the population. If he had encouraged violent methods (as of course he did not), that would probably have so seriously undercut support among whites as to set back work for racial justice for a long time. For King, nonviolence was effective in ways and to a degree that violence could not have been.

Third, *the pragmatic argument reminds us of the great cost of violence*—not mainly in money, but its cost in human lives, in dividing communities more deeply, in leaving a residue of hatred between adversaries, and sometimes in predisposing the losers to resort to violence later on to recover their losses. In Gandhi's nonviolent campaign in India, a violent philosophy and methods might have led to Indian independence. It would, however, have been at a tremendously greater cost to human life and to the fabric of Indian society. Such costs must be figured into all calculations about the relative effectiveness of violent and nonviolent political methods.

At the same time, the pragmatic argument has come under heavy criticism. In a famous essay published in 1940,[10] Reinhold Niebuhr advanced some of these criticisms. First, he wrote, *pragmatic pacifists do not recognize the depth and stubbornness of human sin.* Their faith in the efficacy of nonviolence rests on the belief that all human beings are basically good. They recognize the evil of selfishness, to be sure, but are too confident that it can be overcome by expressions of good will. Thus, he continued, they believe that if Christians had preached love persuasively enough, and if they had refrained from threatening Hitler, he would have been moved by this love and would not have attacked Poland. Human experience, Niebuhr countered, does not justify this optimism. Nor does Christian faith, which recognizes not only the universality of sin but also the depth of people's tendency to deny others' interests when their own power is at stake. He believed that in its rejection of the Christian doctrine of sin, the pragmatic argument is a heresy.

Second, Niebuhr pointed out that *the nonresistance commanded in the New Testament is very different from nonviolent resistance.* The command is, "Do not resist one who is evil" (Matt. 5:39), not "Resist nonviolently those who are evil." The difference is considerable. The first appears to be an ethic that does not seek success in power struggles. The second seeks to win power struggles by nonviolent means.

Third, Niebuhr observed that *pragmatic pacifists in effect give a moral preference to tyranny over war.* They argue that tyranny, if not resisted, will destroy itself from within; and yet, he countered, experience tells us that if it is not resisted, it will grow. A commitment never to use violence may well play into the hands of a tyrant, who has only to threaten war in order to persuade a nonviolent adversary to give in. Pragmatic pacifists, with their absolute rule of nonviolent resistance, assume that war would always be worse in the long run than tyranny. They sometimes argue that the tyranny in question is no worse than the evils of democratic countries. In Niebuhr's opinion, Nazi Germany amply disproved both these judgments. He would likely draw a similar conclusion about Iraq under Saddam Hussein.

Others have offered further criticisms of the pragmatic argument. Kenneth Waltz's analysis of the causes of war[11] implies a fourth criticism. *The decentralized structure of international politics (its lacking an overarching government) makes some occurrence of war likely in spite of efforts to prevent it.* If sin is universal and deep, some unscrupulous governments will seek to take advantage of neighboring countries. There is no world government to restrain the unscrupulous by the peaceful means that can operate within a country. In some cases only a balance of power, along with a willingness to go to war if necessary, can provide security against the unscrupulous. The structure of international politics, Waltz writes, is an underlying framework that permits wars to occur. Within this framework the failings of individuals and of governments make it highly likely that wars will sometimes occur.

A fifth criticism of the pragmatic argument is that *it dogmatically overstates the effectiveness of nonviolence*. Many nonpacifists grant that nonviolence is effective in some situations. It has been effective especially when rulers (or their armies) identify so much with the nonviolent resisters that they are not willing simply to resort to slaughter. This was generally true of the British rulers of India; it was true of the United States government that eventually passed civil rights legislation to support African-Americans' campaign for racial justice; it was true of the Philippine army in 1986 that would not fire on the nonviolent supporters of Mrs. Aquino who were protesting against the government of President Marcos. This condition is much more likely to be present *within* a country than *between* independent countries.

Experience suggests that under some circumstances nonviolence is not likely to be an effective means of protecting people against harm. When an army or its rulers do not value the resisters, they are not likely to refrain from destroying them. So Hitler's troops wiped out the Jews who were offering nonviolent resistance in Warsaw early in the Second World War. Similarly the Romanian government in 1990 brought miners to Bucharest and set them violently upon nonviolent protesters. Especially in the relations between adversary countries, an expansionist power is likely to have few scruples about violently attacking those who resist by any means. Even though Denmark did not offer armed resistance to the Germans in 1940, Nazi rule afterward subjected the Danes to the same kinds of atrocities it inflicted elsewhere.

From such experience, can we expect that nonviolent means alone would provide adequate security for Israel or Kuwait? Only the dogmatic give an assured affirmative answer to this kind of question. It seems more in keeping with experience to refrain from excessive claims for the efficacy of nonviolent resistance.[12]

But if nonviolence is not *always* effective, the pragmatic argument cannot show that violent means, including wars, are *always* wrong. Yet one might be convinced on other grounds that war is always wrong. Let us turn then to an evaluation of the witnessing argument.

2. *Evaluating the witnessing argument*

Some strengths: First, *the witnessing argument does not depend upon any judgment about whether nonviolence is an effective means to peace.* Rather it is that war is always wrong because it is incompatible with a Christian understanding of God and with being a follower of Jesus. A pacifist can offer this argument without regard to whether nonviolence is always a more effective means to a peace than violence.

Second, *witnessing pacifism recognizes that a judgment about pacifism is most basically a theological judgment.* Unlike the pragmatic argument, which argues mainly in psychological and political terms, the witnessing argument makes an essentially theological case. Whether one agrees with it depends, then, upon how one understands the Christian proclamation.

Third, *the witnessing argument takes with great seriousness the strict nature of the Christian life.* It holds that Christian discipleship is a demanding stance, not to be confused with the views of the surrounding society.

Issues concerning the witnessing argument. We can best identify these issues by contrasting witnessing pacifists and just-war thinkers. The latter put questions to witnessing pacifists at three main points: (1) how *agape* love is to be understood, (2) what responsibility Christians should take for what may happen to other people, and (3) how the church is to be understood.

First, *how is agape love to be understood?* Witnessing pacifists believe that love is incompatible with war or any other violence. As we have seen above, Jesus' life and teaching are the model for God's love and thus for the love that God commands in us. The key to the meaning of that love is self-denial, even to the point of cross-bearing, as Jesus exemplified. In the face of attack, then, one is to turn the other cheek, not to strike back.

Just-war thinkers like Paul Ramsey question that understanding of love.[13] In Ramsey's interpretation (which we shall discuss further in chapter 3), love's concern is to meet the needs of our neighbors, or as he later wrote, to keep covenant faithfulness with others. Imagine a case, he says, in which our neighbors' lives are unjustly threatened by a third party—another of one's neighbors. When neighbor attacks neighbor, meeting our neighbors' needs and keeping faithfulness may require, not simply that we refuse to use violence (which would not assist the victims in their plight), but that we stand between victims and wrongdoers, using violence if necessary to protect the oppressed.

A witnessing pacifist like Yoder does not, of course, accept Ramsey's interpretation. Yoder's argument is that one who through faith in God refuses to use violence is the true disciple of Jesus. Ramsey's position is that true discipleship will lead one to resist so as to protect those unjustly attacked. There is no easy resolution of this disagreement. Here are two conscientious, differing Christian interpretations of love.

Second, *should Christians take responsibility to try to prevent unjustifiable, violent attacks upon others?* Yoder and Hauerwas maintain that Christian faith in God means that we must not try to control the course of events. Instead we must adopt a nonviolent style of life that expresses our discipleship. Christians lament the wrongful harm that is done to others, and they side nonviolently with those who are being oppressed; but the unjust harm is someone else's doing, not their own. This argument about responsibility is consistent with the witnessing pacifist's interpretation of love.

A just-war response expresses the different just-war view of love described above. Love's concern is the well-being of our neighbors. Yet some neighbors may seek to harm others. If we do not, from whatever motives, aid intended victims when we could, even if sometimes that aid requires using violence, then we are in part responsible for the evil that we have allowed.

The witnessing pacifist answers that in war, "responsibility" always seems to mean (for just-war thinkers) putting the national interest ahead of the good of other groups, including that of the enemy. Just-war thinkers rejoin that this is true when there is just cause to resist the enemy attack, but not when one's own side is unjust. And on and on the discussion goes—we hope in the spirit of Christian love!

Third, *how is the church to be understood?* For witnessing pacifists like Yoder and Hauerwas, the church seeks to embody the strenuous example and teaching of Jesus in a strict way of life. It presents to the world its own witness of word and works of love, but its members do not try to shape the world by entering into politics and wielding power. The church *is* a social ethic, Hauerwas writes, and it does not have enough in common with those outside the church to deliberate with them about the shape of public policy.

For just-war Christians like Reinhold Niebuhr and Paul Ramsey, the church necessarily influences public policy, and it should. As a social institution the church always affects the wider society, whether its members so intend or not. If they do not enter into public discussion of policy toward defense and war, they are leaving this work to others, and they are in part responsible for the outcome. There is in fact much that Christians and nonChristians can discuss together, as is clear when the subject is, for example, medical ethics. Why can they not deliberate together about public policy when the topic is war?

There is no ready resolution of the disagreement between witnessing pacifists and just-war thinkers. Their differences are rooted in sharply contrasting interpretations of the Christian gospel. Neither can simply dismiss the other as ignorant or insincere. Both positions have arisen out of serious reflection by conscientious Christians. Advocates of both positions are often well-informed about political and military issues. It is fitting then that each pays the other a certain respect. Just-war reasoning, according to Yoder, is "the only serious way of dealing with the moral problem of war apart from pacifism."[14] Witnessing pacifism, Niebuhr writes, is "a valuable asset for the Christian faith."[15] Yet neither position finds in the other an adequate appreciation of its own insight, and the disagreement continues.

In order to highlight issues about witnessing pacifism, we have already begun to discuss just-war thinking, the third kind of response of Christians to war. Let us proceed now to examine that position more directly.

CHAPTER THREE

Just-War Thinking

The Christian Just-War Tradition

As we have seen, when Roman persecution of the church ended in 312 C.E., many Christians began to see the Roman Empire's use of force in a different light. They came to believe that under some conditions it could be justifiable for the state to use force. The first theologians to set forth a Christian theory of justifiable war[1] were Ambrose and Augustine in the late fourth and early fifth centuries.

Augustine's idea of justifiable war arose out of his response to two convictions. The first was that one is obligated not to act out of selfish desire. For that reason he held that it is wrong to kill an attacker simply in order to save one's own life. The second was that there is a duty to act out of the desire to help other people. Therefore the state has an obligation to protect people from the destruction that others do, to avenge injuries, and to restore what has been unjustly taken. Rulers should be prepared to use force, then, to maintain a peaceful and just order in society; and soldiers—servants of the law—can rightly obey a ruler's orders to this end.

In support of this position, Augustine argued that if the Christian religion condemned all wars, the command to soldiers would have been to throw away their arms and leave military service, and it was not (cf. Luke 3:14). Christians are called to be peacemakers (Matt. 5:9), Augustine said; and yet among the peacemakers are also those who wage war in a peaceable spirit to bring back the benefits of peace. When it is simply the self's interests that are at stake, one is to turn the other cheek (Matt. 5:39); but when the danger is to others, then the soldier is inwardly to refrain from selfishness but outwardly to resist, even if that requires taking the attacker's life. Yet Christians will lament even justifiable wars. When fighting them, one should observe certain limits: fight only under rightly constituted authority, refrain from attacking any except wrongdoers, keep one's word even with them, seek no revenge, and show mercy to the defeated and to captives.

Over the years since Augustine, Christian thinkers have developed further the criteria for justifiable war and have related them to the wars of their own periods. The Middle Ages was a time of much warfare among Christians under different kings and nobles. In that situation Gratian, Thomas Aquinas, and others further developed and systematized the criteria, both for justifiable resort to war and for means within war. In the sixteenth and seventeenth centuries, wars of religion and wars against the natives in the New World led theologians to relate the criteria to those troubling events. In our own time, after a period in which just-war thinking was less prominent, theologians have worked to express the just-war criteria in relation to the Second World War, the development of nuclear weapons and strategies of nuclear deterrence, and the other kinds of wars that have been fought in this technological age.

Underlying Convictions of Just-War Thinking

1. Christian just-war thinking arises out of the combination of three convictions. The first is that *God, who is the Creator and Ruler of all, is in covenant with all.*[2] God has created all people to live in community with God, one another, and the natural world. All are called, then, to live as fellow covenant members—neighbors—one with another, trusting in God, and being trustworthy and loving toward others. Because every person is God's, each is called to respect all others as persons, or, to use a modern expres-

sion, as *ends* and not as *means* only. One's neighbors include not only one's friends and allies, but also one's enemies—those who attack us and despitefully use us.

Just-war thinkers share this first conviction with pacifists. This is why the two have a strong basis for discussing their deep differences on war. In contrast, just-war thinkers do not have this kind of common ground with crusaders, who divide people into the righteous and the evil, those on God's side and those who are against God. Instead, just-war thinkers hold that all sides to a dispute embody degrees of justice and injustice. All people are mixtures of good and evil, and yet God loves them all.

2. The second conviction is that *the world is persistently beset by conflicts among people.* Among the persisting social conflicts are those in which some take advantage of others, do them an injustice, destroy them. This is true of individuals and of large groups; of lone criminals and organized crime; of public and private officials who deceive for their own or their group's gain; and of countries that unjustifiably attack others near and far.

Two types of conditions encourage intentional and seriously destructive attack upon others. The first is *sin*—the refusal to live in trust and loyalty with God with others. Sin is universal. All people are prone to be untrustworthy and disloyal, even though that inclination is mixed with its opposite, some degree of trust in God and acceptance of the neighbor. Yet sin does not suffice to explain the worst kinds of destructiveness.

The second type of condition is the social circumstances in which people act. Some circumstances offer strong temptations to be harmful: for example, access to wealth without having to be accountable, or possession of great political power without adequate external checks. The temptation is often greater for large groups than for individuals. A militarily strong country may desire the wealth of its next-door neighbor. The temptation can lead the strong country to demand security against imaginary dangers, or "living space," or revenge, or elimination of "inferior peoples." Wars often follow.

One enduring characteristic of international politics makes it especially prone to war's destruction: there is no world government. When individuals and groups wrong others within a relatively just country, there are procedures and powers to restrain these practices and bring the wrongdoers to justice. In international politics no such world-governmental procedures and powers exist. Whether things would be better or worse under a world government is another question; in any event, none seems possible under foreseeable circumstances. The United Nations can be a valuable forum for discussion and, when enough countries agree, for action to restrain a wrong; but the UN is not a government. The permanent members of the Security Council can act together only as long as each voluntarily cooperates with the others.

These different kinds of circumstances combine to make war likely. The lack of a world government means that there are not adequate sanctions to prevent wars from occurring. Within that framework, people's inclination to take advantage of others, together with political and social conditions that often encourage them to do so, means that wars do in fact sometimes occur.[3]

3. These two convictions lead just-war thinkers to a third: *Christian respect for all God's children sometimes calls for the use of force to protect victims from their attackers.* Paul Ramsey puts it this way: "When choice *must* be made between the perpetrator of injustice and the many victims of it, the latter may and should be preferred." He asks concerning the Parable of the Good Samaritan, "What do you think Jesus would have made the Samaritan do if he had come upon the scene while the robbers were still at their fell work?" (cf. Luke 10:30-37). If only the self's interests are at stake, Ramsey continues (agreeing with Augustine), then one should turn the other cheek. But it is not a work of love to turn the face of another oppressed person to be struck on the other cheek. Instead love bids us interpose ourselves between oppressor and oppressed, even if it requires the use of armed force.[4]

In this third conviction, just-war Christians differ seriously
with witnessing pacifists. Both seek to be guided by *agape* love,
but they interpret what love requires in sharply different ways.
Just-war thinkers believe that love can obligate us to use force to
protect the victims of unjust attack. Love does not merely, as it
were, look aside while we wrongly use force. Nor does it merely
permit the use of force. Sometimes love positively calls for its use
for others' sakes. At the root of a Christian just-war conception of
love is respect for all persons. From that respect comes the effort
to serve their needs, including protecting them from unjust harm.
Love, in a just-war understanding, does not require nonresistance, and not necessarily nonviolent resistance. How one should
oppose injustice is to be shaped by the inner spirit of love and the
circumstances of the injustice. If we always refrain from violent
resistance, we shall have refused to accept our responsibility.

Christian just-war thinking is based, then, on (1) an understanding of God's covenanting love—the kind of love that all people should have toward one another, and (2) recognition of the
persisting, often destructive conflicts of human life. The conclusion is that sometimes war can be justifiable. But just-war
thinkers are not content with that simple conclusion. War can
also be unjustifiable, and more often than not it is, for one reason
or another. It can be fully justifiable only to the extent that it
meets certain criteria.

Just-War Criteria

Just-war teaching includes two sets of criteria. First are criteria
for justifiable *resort* to war (referred to by the Latin phrase, *jus ad
bellum*). Beyond that set is a second—criteria for justifiable
means in war (*jus in bello*). Neither set is reducible to the other. A
country that is justified in resorting to war might nevertheless
fight the war wrongly. Or conversely, it might fight by justifiable
means a war to which it never should have resorted.

Others besides Christians use the just-war criteria. Some political philosophers of other persuasions, secular or religious, also believe that these criteria should govern the resort to and conduct of wars.[5] Their work can help Christian just-war thinkers think about the criteria, in spite of differences over the grounds for using them.

Justifiable Resort to War

The number of just-war criteria for resort to war has increased over time. There is no authoritative or legislated list. Instead these tests are matters of more or less widespread agreement among just-war thinkers. Some contemporary lists include six, some seven, some more.

1. *Justifiable cause.* This is the most fundamental of the criteria for resort to war. Without it the others do not even come into play. "Just cause" refers to a valid reason for resorting to war. Such a reason arises out of some wrong that has been done or is about to be done, a wrong that is to be repaired or prevented. Traditionally, the types of just cause have been (1) to protect people from unjust attack, (2) to restore rights that have wrongly been taken away, and (3) to defend or reestablish a just political order.

Just-war thinkers have held that a just cause is usually present in a defensive war—in the effort to resist an enemy attack. That judgment is ordinarily plausible. Yet two qualifications are needed. First, protecting people from unjust attack may sometimes justify a preemptive strike—attacking first in the face of an imminent enemy invasion. A vivid example occurred in 1967, when Israeli intelligence learned that Egypt and Syria were at the point of attacking, with the possibility that the state of Israel would be destroyed. The Israelis, by an air assault shortly beforehand, destroyed the Arab air forces on the ground and thereby prevented a possible Arab victory. Second, not all defensive wars are justifiable. Hitler's persecution of Jews under his rule in the 1930s might have been a just cause for initiating war against Germany. If so, it would be morally perverse to claim that Germany would have had a just cause because of fighting a defensive war. When a country is defending its right to continue committing atrocities, self-defense is no longer a just cause. It is not self-defense as such that is justifiable, but the righting of a grave wrong or the defense of a fundamental right.

Consider further the idea that it is not necessarily wrong to initiate a war. One could say that the Persian Gulf War began when the coalition launched an attack, and that Iraq was at that point fighting a defensive war. Yet whether the coalition had just cause would depend upon other grounds, such as whether it should have attacked to restore the rights of Kuwait, which Iraq had unjustly invaded; and whether attacking Iraq was essential to reestablish a more just order in the region and to protect it from further Iraqi military action. People of good will have argued on both sides of those questions, but questions like those are crucial, and not simply who initiated the shooting.

Just cause does not mean that one side's cause is pure and that the other's lacks any merit. That notion is more akin to the crusade of the righteous against the forces of evil. Whenever a country protects people from unjust attack, or restores their rights, or defends a just order, it does so at best as a matter of degrees of justice. It likely is protecting a somewhat unjust society from attack. It may restore some rights but continue to deprive people of other rights. The order it defends is never a perfectly just order. But the absence of moral purity does not make vain all moral judgments about war. A difference of degree can have great moral significance. Even though Finland in 1939 was not (I assume) a perfectly just society, the Soviet Union's attack was a vastly greater injustice. Similarly, even though Kuwait in 1990 was not a fully just society, Iraq's attack was by far the worse injustice. As Reinhold Niebuhr argued in 1940, the relevant judgment is not that all alike, Hitler and the Allies, are sinners. Rather it is that some of those sinners are responsible for far greater destruction and injustice than others.

Like the other criteria, judgments about just cause are disputable. Conscientious and well-informed people will often disagree about them. That cannot be avoided. What is important is that the criterion of just cause take center-stage in the discussion: What unjust harm has been done or is being done or will likely be done? What is at stake for the wider political order?

Just cause is a necessary but not a sufficient condition for justifiable resort to war. Its presence does not suffice to make resort to war right, but its absence is enough to make it wrong. Whether resort to war is fully justifiable depends upon whether all the other criteria for resort are met.

2. *Legitimate authority.* The issue here is "Who should decide?" What is at stake is that justifiable resort to war must serve public and not merely private purposes. The decision must therefore be made by those who bear the responsibility to decide for the people. In the Middle Ages this criterion prohibited private armies from conducting their own wars and enveloping the society in chaos. In our time it requires that the decision be deliberated and made at the highest levels of government. Those who decide must be held responsible for their decision, and that can happen when they are required to offer and justify their reasons. It is not enough for a leader to involve a country in war and say, in effect, "Trust me." At some level the judgment must be subjected to examination. Otherwise the leader might be following whims, private passions, likes and dislikes, compulsions. The legitimate authorities are required to give an appropriate account of their reasons.

Those in legitimate authority must decide for the country. At the same time citizens must decide for themselves—decide whether they are prepared to support the government's decision as right. Private citizens are usually not in as good a position to decide. They lack adequate information about the wider context, they will not be held responsible in the same way, and they may be preoccupied by the impact of the decision on their private pursuits. For such reasons, the just-war tradition has held that citizens should presume that legitimate authorities, if they have followed proper procedures, have decided rightly. There may, however, be good reason to conclude otherwise. Before private citizens reach that conclusion, however, they should try to imagine themselves in the situation of the authorities—look at the wider picture, ask what would happen if this or if that, and imagine that they will be held responsible by the public for their judgments. Justifiable decisions about war are decisions about the public good, within and beyond one's own country.

3. *Last resort.* It is justifiable to resort to war only after all peaceful alternatives to war have been exhausted without success. A government ought not enter into the destruction that war entails if there is a reasonable chance of attaining its just objectives by less destructive measures.

When last resort has been reached is a matter of judgment. If a government literally tried every imaginable possibility before resort to war, it would often make it impossible—or far more difficult—to serve its just cause. When Neville Chamberlain accepted Hitler's terms at Munich in 1938, he supposed that Hitler was acting in good faith and that the agreement could prevent war. Others judged at the time that Hitler's promises were worthless and that last resort had already been reached. Hindsight has supported those judgments. Last resort requires a considered judgment about whether some imagined alternative has a good chance of avoiding war. It does not require that every idea actually be pursued to the end of the line. That would only play into the hands of a skillful and determined adversary.

A controversial issue concerning the United States' resort to war against Iraq was whether last resort had been reached. That case illustrates the difficulty of deciding about last resort. Some judged that negotiation with President Saddam Hussein might yet bring an acceptable solution short of war. Others pointed to the vigorous efforts that many parties had made to mediate the conflict, without the slightest concession from Iraq. A second kind of argument was that the blockade of Iraq had not had enough time to work—that it could eventually bring about Iraq's withdrawal from Kuwait short of war. The questions this issue raises are daunting: How much time would be enough? Would the blockade hold, or might Iran or some other country allow Iraq to import what it needed? Would not a continued blockade be especially harmful to Iraqi civilians, and not only to political and military leaders? Could the coalition confronting Iraq hold together over a long period? Would the lengthy presence of Western, non-Islamic troops in Saudi Arabia alienate allied Moslem countries? Would the summer desert environment erode the coalition's military equipment and the troops' morale? Might the Iraqis develop and deploy nuclear weapons in the interim? Had the Bush administration adequately explained its reasons for proceeding to military action? Were there good reasons why some relevant considerations could not be discussed in public?

Decisions about last resort cannot be exact. Awareness of the many factors and information about the actual circumstances will help, but intuition and one's predispositions will always play a role in the outcome. Here again conscientious and well-informed persons will often disagree. That does not diminish the importance of this criterion. Governments must always seek alternatives to war as long as they hold out reasonable promise.

4. *Declaration of war aims.* Some lists of just-war criteria include the requirement of a formal declaration of war. Depending upon the country, that may be legally required. It announces one's aims to the world, including the enemy. Sometimes, however, a formal declaration is not feasible prior to military action, and some argue that it is not always morally obligatory. In the Six-Day War in 1967, for example, if the Israelis had declared war beforehand, they could not have surprised the Egyptian and Syrian air forces on the ground. According to this argument, if the Israelis were justified in launching a preemptive attack to prevent destruction of their country, they were also justified in not tipping off the enemy ahead of time.

James Childress has proposed a variation from the requirement to declare war.[6] He writes that a formal declaration of war is an extension of the criterion of last resort, because it is the last opportunity short of war to persuade the enemy to come to terms. Even when a formal declaration is not appropriate, he continues, a declaration of war *aims* should be made, to explain and justify the resort to arms to the public. One can add that declaring war aims requires a government to reflect on the outcome it seeks in a war. Also in a democracy, declaring war aims brings the public intentionally into the deliberative process, and it creates a stated commitment to the declared aims.

5. *Proportionality*. This criterion prohibits resort to war if the evil effects of doing so will likely exceed the evil to be prevented (and the good to be attained) by going to war. This criterion requires a reasonable calculation of consequences, "counting the cost," even though that is not easy. Matters of proportionality helped lead the United States government to favor the British and French over the Axis powers prior to Pearl Harbor. President Roosevelt thought that the world, and not only the United States, would be far worse off if the Axis powers won. It would have been wise, many say, for the United States to have counted the cost more fully prior to its deep military involvement in Vietnam. Proportionality is a simple rule of common sense: not only is it morally wrong to make matters worse; it also makes no sense.

Sometimes we are told that because it is impossible to calculate consequences adequately, we ought to put this criterion aside. In response, just-war thinkers grant that we cannot calculate consequences well. They also hold that this criterion is perhaps not the foremost limit on resort to war. Yet, they continue, it is better to calculate consequences the best we can, however imperfectly, than not to do so at all. People are apparently guided by that belief in private life. We often ask of an act, like changing jobs, or buying a car, or enlisting in the military, "What might happen if we do that?" Best that we do ask that, even though our forecasts are far from perfect.

Calculating proportionality about the Persian Gulf War meant asking both "What will happen if we attack?" and "What will happen if we do not?" It also involved more complex questions, such as "What if we maintain the blockade for a year without attacking?" and "What if this combination of allies attacks rather than that combination?" Strategists usually respond to these questions, not with the simple answer that this will happen, or that. Rather they identify an array of possible outcomes and try to assess the likelihood of each. They give special attention to likely outcomes and to ones that are highly undesirable, even if unlikely. Thinking about proportionality takes that form today. It is not easy, but just-war thinkers say that the effort is morally required.

6. *Reasonable chance of success.* In just-war thinking it is not right to resort to war unless there is a reasonable chance of attaining one's justifiable objectives. This is an extension of the test of proportionality.

The idea of "success" in war can easily fall victim to crusade thinking. That happens when "success" is taken to mean simply "victory," and when that term is translated into total military defeat of the enemy. "Success" is better seen, not merely as total military victory, but as effectively attaining the war's just objectives. If the western allies in the Second World War had thought more seriously about their war aims, they might have sought a stable balance to Soviet power in central Europe. Without much thought about that, they helped defeat Germany so thoroughly as to produce a precarious balance in Europe between the West and the Soviet Union for decades thereafter.

That example is instructive for the Persian Gulf War as well. A war aim of complete destruction of Iraq as a military power could have created further instability in the Middle East, with Iran, Syria, and others vying to replace Iraqi influence. That would have undercut what should be a long-range goal of any war—a more just and enduring peace.

It is needful to ask, then, "Success of what justifiable sort?" Reasonable chance of success in the Gulf War then meant a reasonable chance of bringing about the objectives the coalition should have had for the war.

7. *Right intention.* The term "intention" here is to be understood in two ways. First, it refers to the motives for action. Even if there is a just cause, the war must not be waged out of hatred for the enemy, nor from the desire for revenge. Rather, when Christians go to war, they are to do so out of love for their enemies, as well as for the victims involved.

This first sense shapes the second, in which "intention" refers to the objective of one's action—what one should seek to accomplish. The objective of war should always be a better and more just peace. It should never be killing and destruction as such. "Right intention" is a way of saying that war is never rightly an end in itself, never justifiably an activity separable from moral examination. When war is justifiable, it is only as a means to peace. So the motives and aims of war are to be governed by the goal of a just peace.

While right intention is a test for justifiable resort to war, it also underlies the criteria for justifiable conduct of war, to which we now turn.[7]

Justifiable Means in War

In just-war teaching, Christian love shapes and limits what it is right to do in war, and not only on the way to war. It does so through two criteria.

1. *The principle of discrimination.* This criterion illustrates most clearly the close connection between right intention and the means of war. Whether one observes the principle of discrimination reveals whether one's real objective is a better peace, or whether it is simply to kill and destroy. It shows whether one considers all those of the enemy country to be God's children, like oneself, or merely evils to be stamped out or obstacles to be eliminated. Discrimination between morally permissible and

impermissible targets is an essential sign of a Christian moral outlook upon war.

The principle of discrimination *forbids direct and intentional attack upon noncombatants in war*. The basic concepts here need explanation.

a. *Noncombatants* are all who are not close participants in doing military acts that must be restrained in war. Combatants are those who are close participants in such military acts. To put it most simply, combatants are military personnel and their commanders (military or civilian) who are not prisoners. Civilians who are not in the line of command, along with prisoners, are noncombatants.

This distinction hinges upon a person's role, not one's loyalties or attitudes. Being a loyal supporter of the enemy's war effort does not make one a combatant. If it did, nearly all people above the age of six could be thought combatants. But that is not what combatancy means. A combatant is someone whose role is either carrying out a military act, such as firing a gun, or cooperating closely in the act, such as driving the armed vehicle from which others are firing the gun or training to do actions like those. A noncombatant is anyone who is not closely cooperating in military acts as such.

Noncombatants include all those whose roles are to serve the needs of the person as person, rather than the needs of military action as such.[8] So medical personnel at the front are noncombatants, as are chaplains. Bakers who deliver food to an army are noncombatants, because people must eat whether they are in uniform or not. In any city, most people are noncombatants; most either carry out roles that are needed in ordinary, nonmilitary life, or they are small children, the unemployed, or the elderly. The fire-bombing of Dresden and Tokyo in 1945 was aimed at civilians, not mainly at military targets. The civilian population of Hiroshima and Nagasaki greatly outnumbered the military personnel, and the choice of these cities as targets was in large part because of their size and relative lack of prior damage, so that the power of the atom bombs would be apparent. Mr. Truman called them "military targets" because he and his advisors had lost sight of the combatant/noncombatant distinction.

The very point of justifiable war—to prevent or repair some grave wrong—explains why noncombatants should be exempt from direct and intentional attack. They are not the doers of the wrong to be restrained. Therefore they have a right to immunity from intentional attack.

There are borderline cases, of course, but one cannot begin to think about a borderline case unless one has grasped the reason for the distinction. What about those who work in arms factories, for example? If the reason for using force is to prevent a grave wrong, one does that most directly by attacking military forces. If a war is not going to be very short, one also does it by striking factories that produce weapons, but that does not always entail attacking the people who make them. A conscience informed by love for the enemy does not easily broaden the target to include borderline cases when the war's just objective can be served as well by restricted targeting.

b. An *intentional* attack is to be distinguished from an *unintended side effect*. In this context, one's intention refers to what one is trying to accomplish, that is, what and whom one is seeking to harm. At Dresden and Tokyo, Hiroshima and Nagasaki, the intent was to harm civilians, and not only military targets in the proper sense of the term. That is prohibited by the principle of discrimination.

The principle does not prohibit all harm to noncombatants. An air raid in Iraq, say, was upon a military installation, and some civilians who happened to live nearby were killed in the process. If the objective was the military installation, not the civilians, that was not an intentional attack upon them. If they were part of the objective, the attack on them was intentional. Even if the intent is not to harm civilians, an attack on a military target is prohibited if civilian casualties are likely to be disproportionately high. In recent years, just-war thinkers have said that refraining from intending civilian deaths is not enough; one must also seek to *avoid* harming civilians. Intention in this sense is not merely an internal matter. It also has an external, objective dimension, built into the shape of the act. So it was not possible to aim fire bombs at residential areas of Dresden without objectively intending civilian deaths.

c. A *direct* attack here refers to one that aims at noncombatants as a way of getting at the military. It is not sufficient that the ultimate targets are military. Noncombatants have a right not to be used as mere means to getting at combatants. This rules out using civilians or prisoners of war as hostages and placing them at sites likely to be attacked. It condemns holding a gun to the head of a criminal's child in order to coerce the criminal into surrendering. It prohibits torture of prisoners of war to get useful military information. It forbids attacks on enemy cities to undermine morale (even if this were the effect, which military studies have found it was often not).

2. *Proportionality.* This is the simplest of the two criteria for means in war, though as we shall see, it operates only within limits set by the principle of discrimination.

Not only must the condition of proportionality be met before resorting to war. It must also be satisfied repeatedly during the war. Let us assume, for example, that it was justifiable and proportionate for the United States to resort to war against Japan after Pearl Harbor. Even so, that would not settle the question of proportionality about such things as the attack on Tarawa or the use of nuclear weapons. One must assess proportionality over and over again during a war.

The idea of proportionality is reflected in the strategic principle of the economy of force, which calls for the most effective use of one's available forces. On the one hand, the economy of force bids one use the level of force that is required to bring about a justifiable objective. On the other, and equally as important, it rules out using more force than necessary, by applying such tactics as outflanking movements, surprise, and change of the direction of attack. To express a right intention, proportionality requires more than merely achieving one's objectives at the lowest cost in lives and resources for one's own side. Rather proportionality calls for the least destruction possible for all concerned.

One can rightly apply the criterion of proportionality, however, only within limits set by the principle of discrimination. The latter asks what targets it is morally permissible to attack. Proportionality then calls for attacking them effectively with the least possible destruction. Discrimination constitutes a circle, we might say, that sets limits for morally permissible acts in war. Proportionality operates only within that circle. As one does not rightly ask how many people it is proportionate to torture, so one does not ask whether it is proportionate to attack a schoolyard full of children. Discrimination prohibits doing those things at all.

These then are the just-war criteria. Applying them, it may be possible to judge some wars justifiable. By the same logic, some wars—probably most—will be judged unjustifiable in various respects. In the judging, both sets of criteria are obligatory. Justifiable resort to war does not license the use of unlimited means, nor do permissible means make a war right that should never have been fought at all. From Christian faith one knows that limits are required in war because all those on both sides are one's neighbors in Christ. The very existence of such a serious and unavoidable conflict is a matter of deep regret. Therefore one seeks at every point to restrain the destruction in behalf of a more just peace.

Strengths and Weaknesses of Christian Just-War Thinking

1. *Some strengths*

First, *just-war thinking recognizes the persistence of conflict among people, especially in international politics.* Human groups repeatedly struggle with one another, sometimes nonviolently and sometimes violently. Some degree of conflict is to be expected, because the resources that people seek are limited. But conflict will often be much more intense and destructive than necessary because of the universality of sin.

Second, *a just-war approach takes seriously the moral perplexity that arises when resorting to war is the only effective way to restrain grave wrongdoing.* When some countries are riding roughshod over the lives of others, and when going to war is the only way to prevent this, we face a moral perplexity. Is it better to allow the injustice, or to prevent or reverse it at the cost of war's destruction? The just-war tradition recognizes the difficulty of choices in which there are strong moral claims on both sides.

Third, *just-war thinking considers many subsidiary moral questions within the larger issue of war.* This approach sees the need to make moral decisions at every point in the process of responding to war, such as whether to resort to war, by what means, and whether to pursue the war any further.

2. Issues concerning just-war thinking

One question to put to a just-war approach is *whether it merely serves as a rationalization for whatever the government does.* That can happen. Some citizens or national leaders may use the criteria as a check list to try to show that at every point a war is justifiable, but without any serious moral self-examination. When this happens, the criteria have been reduced merely to verbal weapons against those who disagree.

This is misuse of the criteria, not an inherent weakness of a just-war approach. Its thinkers have developed their outlook and their criteria to impose moral limits on war and to hold people morally accountable, not to give them excuses for wrongdoing. When just-war thinkers do their work well, they make moral judgments that cut both ways. Uses of the criteria sometimes call the policies and practices of a war into question, and sometimes they indicate that a policy or practice is morally permissible.

There have been many instances of just-war criticisms of a

government's military practices. Here are three examples: In the midst of the Second World War, Fr. John C. Ford published an outspoken critique of the Allies' intentional attacks upon German and Japanese cities. He argued that city-bombing is intentional bombing of civilians, and that it is prohibited by the principle of discrimination.[9] A second is Dr. Robert C. Batchelder's examination of the United States decisions to produce the atom bomb and to use two of them against Japan. His careful moral reflection assists theological specialists and nonspecialists alike to see how the United States' use of the atom bombs went beyond the limits of justifiable means.[10] Still another is the work of Paul Ramsey, who in the 1960s examined many aspects of war, such as nuclear deterrence strategy, so as to propose what is morally permitted, what is not, and why.[11]

Just-war considerations also affect countries' actions about war. Franklin Roosevelt's decisions in 1939–1941 were strongly influenced by his belief that the cause of Britain and France was more just than that of Nazi Germany. Increased public attention to the principle of discrimination in recent years influenced the choice of bombing targets in Iraq. The criteria also can have some influence in dictatorships. After the Second World War, we learned of cases in which some German generals, not themselves Nazis, refused to kill prisoners of war and refused to pass on orders that they judged to be morally wrong. Just-war criteria never affect policy as much as we would hope, but in the twentieth century they have had some effect.

Nevertheless this question is important. It bids us take the purpose of the just-war criteria seriously. These criteria exist to help us find a morally justifiable response to situations of moral perplexity about war. When used rightly, they undercut self-righteous efforts to justify one's own side. They also undercut the opposite bias—using the criteria simply as a device to condemn every war in turn. The criteria are not properly tools for people with closed minds. They exist to encourage moral wisdom in difficult situations.

A second question is *whether there can be a justifiable war in this technological age.* In an age of technological weaponry, is it possible any longer for war to be proportionate, or will the destruction inevitably outweigh a just cause? Further, is it possible with technological weapons to discriminate between non-combatants and combatants? It is not only nuclear weapons that raise these questions, but also long-range missiles, chemical and bacteriological weapons, and new kinds of conventional weapons. Practices like the area bombing of the Second World War and the destruction of villages in Vietnam by B-52s have intensified the questions.

On the other hand, a remarkable thing about the Persian Gulf War was the precision of computer- and laser-guided projectiles. They were able to hit their targets with a precision far surpassing any previous war, sometimes from considerable distances. If the question is whether war *can* meet the criteria, the prospect is that further technological development will make discrimination and proportion more possible, rather than less. The more serious question is whether it *will*. That depends more on those who use the weapons than on the weapons themselves. The allied bombing of Iraq, while it sought to be discriminate, appears to have caused a considerable number of civilian deaths and much destruction of nonmilitary structures. Even when the damage to noncombatants is unintended, the principle of proportionality requires that the attacker restrict it as far as possible.

We might rephrase the issue. It is not so much whether there *can* be a justifiable war in this technological age, as whether a war *will* actually be justifiable. The answer is not clear, but the question places the burden where it belongs—on those who make decisions about war, not mainly on technology.

Some go beyond this question to argue that just-war thinking is no longer relevant. Those who claim this, however, often appeal to criteria like proportionality or discrimination to support their argument. Yet an appeal to just-war criteria actually demonstrates their continued relevance. Evaluating wars is exactly what just-war thinking is about. Others say that the only wars that could be just are those of third-world powers against oppressors. Any argument for that view would need to offer criteria more or less like those of the just-war tradition, and careful criteria might justify other kinds of wars.

Third is the question *whether any war today can be justifiable except a war of defense against attack.* Some argue that the weapons are so destructive that there can be no just cause except self-defense. Others have responded that it can still be justifiable, after an aggressor has finished conquering another country, for third parties to initiate another war to throw out the invader, as in the case of the coalition's expelling Iraq from Kuwait. Still others say that sometimes dictators do such atrocities to their own people that it may be right to invade in order to stop them.

A fourth question is *whether the just-war criteria themselves are adequate.* The criteria have never been fixed. Over the centuries they have been continually reexamined in an effort to make them more applicable to existing conditions. Today a number of questions are asked about the criteria: for example, what makes an attack intentional or unintentional, whether we can make meaningful calculations of proportionality, whether in just-war thinking the moral presumption is against the use of force or against injustice, and whether a declaration of war is morally required.

Last, there is the issue *whether just-war thinking as such is an adequate way to think about war.* On one side this question poses an issue between just-war thinkers and crusaders. Should Christians support moral limits in wars against highly unjust regimes? As we have seen, crusaders recognize no moral obligations toward those on the enemy side. This raises the question whether God is the God of all, rather than only of our side; and whether people fit into neat good/evil categories. If one opts for a crusade instead of just-war thinking, there is danger of discarding Christian insights and commitments, as well as diminishing the chances for restraint in war.

On the other side, the issue persists between just-war thinkers and pacifists. Can war ever be an expression of faith in God, loyal discipleship to Jesus Christ, and love for all one's neighbors? As we have seen in chapter 2, just-war thinkers and witnessing pacifists disagree deeply over what faith and discipleship and love require. They will likely go on disagreeing into the far future. Yet discussion between the two positions is well worth conducting. It is about what it means to be Christians and what constitutes a justifiable response toward those who do dire evils to others.

John Howard Yoder, a witnessing pacifist, has said that if he cannot persuade others to be pacifists, then he would like for them to be good just-war thinkers. At least they would then be disposed to impose moral restraints on violence. And many just-war thinkers believe that their closest allies over the morality of war are not the crusaders, who agree with them that it can sometimes be justifiable to go to war. Rather they are witnessing pacifists, who recognize the universal rule of God, Christians' obligation to all God's children, and the persistence of destructive conflict.

CHAPTER FOUR

What Can We Do?

Someone has said that war is too important to leave to the generals. It is also too important to leave to presidents and parliaments. The public provides the people who fight wars, it pays the bills, and it undergoes the major social changes that wars bring. Ordinary citizens need to think carefully about war and then to take appropriate action. This concluding chapter discusses what appropriate action might be in response to war.

General Observations

Several presuppositions shape the suggestions offered here.

1. I am here speaking mainly to Christians. This book has throughout discussed war in relation to the Christian tradition, has shown ways that each approach has appealed to that tradition, and has evaluated each from a Christian standpoint. When Christians discuss war in relation to Christian belief, they affirm that it too is an issue for faith. They show that it is important to discuss controversial matters over which they disagree. Those discussions may both help anchor their own convictions and increase their appreciation for other Christians who conscientiously disagree with them.

It is also worthwhile for Christians to discuss war with nonChristians. Christians bring much in common to the discussion with those who have other outlooks: life in the same political community, similar fears and hopes about war's outcome, and shared experiences of life that make it possible to discuss the reasons for our agreements and disagreements. I do not agree with those who claim that there is no ground for talking about war with people who do not share the same faith. We make moral judgments about other subjects (like truth-telling, medical treatment, and policies in the workplace) that nonChristians can understand and assess. That is also possible with war.

2. I am also speaking primarily to those who live in democracies, where those who would rule must gain office through competition for votes, and where there is freedom of speech, with the right to dissent. Citizens of democracies have some influence, however indirect, over government policies. In this they differ from the early Christians, who had only the choices of accepting or rejecting their subjection to the governing authorities (Rom. 13:1). They differ also from those today living under autocratic rule, who can have little influence over their rulers except through revolution. The responses discussed below presuppose a democratic framework.

3. Not all citizens have the same responsibilities toward war. A few are directly involved in molding their country's policies toward war; in their offices they carry a special burden of responsibility. Others, as in the military, are legally obligated to carry out policies they did not make and with which they may or may not agree. When they conscientiously agree, they still face grave dangers and may be called upon to sacrifice their lives. When they conscientiously disagree, they encounter special difficulties in deciding what they should do. But most adults are ordinary citizens going about their usual nonmilitary pursuits. In a democracy they have the opportunity and the duty to influence what is done. It is to these ordinary citizens that I am especially speaking here.

4. In any country there are severe limits on the influence of individuals and groups. Democratic governments respond to the voices and votes of millions of people. What any group demands

will conflict with the wishes of others and often with what is wise or even possible. Elected leaders—including presidents— also work under serious limits as they seek to make policy. They do not simply give orders; much of their effort goes into per- suading, cajoling, explaining, bargaining—working within the limits imposed by the size and complexity and pluralism of gov- ernment. And beyond a country's boundaries lies a world that it can change only somewhat. Citizens in a democracy can have some influence on wars, and they share in responsibility for what happens, but their power is seriously restricted.

5. Christians often disagree, not only about resort to war and means in war, but also about how they as citizens should act in response to war. Their disagreements about action tend to paral- lel their different moral stances toward war. Crusaders are likely to propose one set of responses, pacifists another, and just-war thinkers still another. Further, pragmatic pacifists and witnessing pacifists may offer different action proposals, and those who by just-war criteria think a war justifiable will propose different responses from those who by the same criteria think it wrong. Christians need to avoid presuming that their action proposals are morally self-evident. They are no stronger than the stances toward war out of which they arise. In the following section I shall indi- cate some of the connections between stance and proposals for action.

Some Responses Christians Can Make

1. *Prayer*. Crusaders, confident that they are fighting for God's cause and that their adversaries are evil, express their views in praying with Deborah, "So perish all your enemies, O Lord!" (Judges 5:31). They pray for war not to come, but when it does, for strength to continue the fight until the forces of evil are thor- oughly defeated, and for a peace that will long endure.

Pacifists, convinced that it is always wrong to go to war, and believing (many of them) that war is the worst evil that people can inflict, show their convictions in praying for peace, that war not begin, and that present wars will come to a speedy end with the least possible destruction. They pray for strength to persist in their opposition to war in the face of strong pressures to support it, for the people on both sides, and for opportunities to do works of love and justice in spite of killing and destruction.

Just-war advocates, believing that some wars are justifiable and some are not, reflect their convictions when they pray for wisdom to discern the difference and for persistence in doing what they believe is right. When they support a war, they pray for enemies as well as for allies, for firmness and yet restraint in defending and advancing a more just cause, and for the absence of vindictiveness. When they oppose a war, they pray for effective ways to declare their convictions and for a change of heart by those who conduct the war. Whether they support or oppose, they pray for an early and more just peace and for effective avenues to bind up the wounds on all sides. Seeing the war as one between more and less just causes, they pray for deliverance from self-righteousness and for openness to correction.

2. *Repentance.* Repentance is appropriate both for our sins and our sin: for the wrongs we have done, and for the underlying rebelliousness against God and neighbor out of which those wrongs arise. Repentance is concrete, not abstract. It involves recognizing specific ways in which our own actions may have contributed to an evil we deplore—how we have supported practices that in their injustice may have made wars more likely. Repentance is repeatedly in order. Each new day brings new failings in our loyalty to God and neighbor, as well as new awareness that our repentance for past wrongs was not complete.

Repentance is appropriate in time of war whenever we have done such wrongs as these: when we have lacked the courage of our convictions, have not been open to learn from those with whom we differ, have not been willing to risk ourselves to protect or give aid to the victims of war, have ignored injustices present in the cause that we believe to be relatively more just, have been interested only in the welfare of those nearest and dearest to us, have desired to profit from the misfortunes of others, or have longed for a return to life as usual without the burden of care and concern for those who suffer.

In the midst of our repentance God assures us of forgiveness. God welcomes our turning from our wrongs as the father welcomed back the prodigal son. Yet forgiveness is not "cheap grace." True repentance involves "intending to lead a new life, following the commandments of God." It leads us to seek reconciliation with our adversaries—in war, in injustice that breeds wars, and in conflicts over our opinions about war.

3. *Seeking a character befitting a follower of Christ.* Good works arise from a good character, from being inwardly disposed to faith in God and love toward the neighbor. What constitutes love is, however, something over which Christians often disagree. Pacifists believe that the willingness to use violence is never compatible with the love of Christ. Love as they view it is a disposition that in all circumstances does good rather than harm to the neighbor.

Just-war Christians equally seek the character fitting to discipleship, but they interpret that character differently. For them love requires seeking the good of all our neighbors, but we must often do that amid intense conflicts. In those cases, love toward all requires seeking to protect victims from their oppressors, rather than allowing the oppression to continue. A loving character may then be expressed in the restrained use of force.

Even though pacifists and just-war advocates disagree in these ways over the content of Christian character, they share the recognition that being a disciple is a matter of one's character, and not merely an array of right actions. It requires being disposed to seek the good of the neighbor in all our relationships.

4. *Reflecting as Christians upon our lives.* In a crisis we may learn who we are more readily than in ordinary times. When much is at stake, we may suddenly realize the triviality of some pursuits and reorder our priorities.

For some, this may bring a realization of how much our individual lives are bound up with the wider society. Some may hear new callings: new work, new kinds of voluntary service, a new sense of purpose in an old activity.

For Christians, a crisis can be an occasion for exploring anew the wisdom of faith. What follows from saying that God is the Creator of all? What does it mean that "the nations are like a drop from a bucket, and are accounted as dust on the scales" (Isa. 40:15)? Why do some people suffer all out of proportion to their wrongdoing? How inclusive is God's covenant? What is implied by our being in covenant with those with whom we are at war? Is it possible both to forgive our enemies and to resist them, or must we choose the one or the other? In what form are we called to take up a cross?

Reflection need not be an escape from action. Rather it can motivate us anew, redirect our actions, and help us to know our own identity in the midst of our acting.

5. *Encouraging dialogue among Christians about war.* Dialogue is different from propaganda. Propagandists are sure they are right and feel no need to learn further; they seek only to win others over, not to hear. Nothing is so frustrating as to be accosted by somebody in a propagandizing mood. We have the feeling of being manipulated, of not being respected. And nothing is so futile as a debate between two opposing propagandists. They pass as ships in the night, neither perceiving the other. They oversimplify the options and overlook the subtleties. That does not edify, and it divides the participants.

In dialogue, people openly examine their differences in the context of what they hold in common. They allow "the being and truth of each" to confront "the being and truth of the other."[1] In dialogue Christians who disagree about war can come together to express their differences without caricaturing the other's point of view, without being afraid to learn from the other, and without feeling that either must change the other's mind. Each refrains from charging that the other is not a "true Christian." Each can state a conviction without being suspected of trying to speak for the congregation. A sensitive pastor or layperson can moderate the discussion even after making known his or her own convictions, insofar as all perceive the moderator to be fair. In dialogue, all can discuss seriously without falling into the trap of having to arrive at consensus, for in that effort the reservations of some are too readily sacrificed to the drive to appear unified. Through dialogue a group gains inner strength, and at the same time its individual members deepen their insight into strong and weak points in their own positions. They can become more truthful and more chastened in their efforts to affect the wider society.

6. *Strengthening those who suffer in time of war.* War brings pain near and far. Few of us can directly serve people at a great distance, but many can assist those near at hand.

Perhaps we can help children to cope with world events that bewilder and frighten them. Their fears are real, even if not always realistic. We can listen caringly as they express those fears. We need not argue away each fear or give them many facts. Mainly we need to let them speak, to hear them, and to assure them of our loving support.

Or we can support those who have loved ones away at war. Those at home may be fearful and alone. They may have difficulty tending to home and work when a spouse is far away. War strikes unevenly in any community. For some life goes on almost as before; for others it is turned upside down. Some of us can offer our presence and our comfort to those in crisis.

People in the war zone suffer far more than those elsewhere. Those who live in relative comfort at a distance can seek ways to assist the immediate victims of the war. Depending on the circumstances, this may be possible through church or nonchurch relief agencies, the Red Cross, or direct individual contacts, either during or after the war.

7. *Seeking to influence governmental policy.* Christians' convictions about a war will lead many to try to influence their government's policies. In those efforts several cautions are in order.

Some cautions are in behalf of effectiveness. Those who write their representatives will usually be taken more seriously if they are well-informed about the subject and show that they are thinking for themselves. Congressional and White House staffs readily see through organized barrages of identical letters. We are well advised not to threaten ("Do this or I'll vote against you"). If we have good reasons for what we want, we should explain them.

If we are organizing a protest demonstration, we will be wise to do so in a way that does not alienate the persons we hope to influence. It only angers others when we misrepresent their viewpoints. It is repellent to hear charges that those who disagree with us are disloyal or hypocrites. Some demonstrations turn off the very people they hope to influence. Others by their demeanor and effective organization invite sympathy and favor.

Another caution is about fairness. In their public declarations, church advocates of one position or another toward war have sometimes portrayed themselves as representing a greater consensus of church opinion than they do. They have sometimes sought to prevent other church people from voicing competing viewpoints. In these ways they adopt the tactics of many secular pressure groups. Even when we are utterly convinced that we are right, it is still obligatory to be fair. We would often be better advised to advance our views through voluntary, unofficial groups, than to presume to speak for many who on conscientious grounds disagree with us.

8. *Educating for peacemaking.* "Blessed are the peacemakers" (Matt. 5:9). But how do we make peace? We can distinguish two senses of peace. One is the narrow sense—the absence of war. The other, broader sense, is peace as a condition of just and harmonious relationships with God, with one another, and with the natural world. This meaning carries overtones of unity and concord, but also of completeness and delight in God's creation.[2]

Without peace as the absence of war, peace as just concord is not fully present. One way to seek peace in the broader sense, then, is to work for peace in the narrower sense. But the world might be without war and still not have peace as just concord, and the absence of justice might encourage wars to occur. Working for peace in the narrower sense then calls for, among other things, enhancing peace as just concord.

One can speak of peacemakers in either context. Let us focus here especially upon peacemaking in the sense of bringing about a condition without war—one important step in working for peace as just concord. How can we work for peace as the absence of war? Pacifists and just-war advocates often disagree over this issue. They do have some common ground: they can both recognize the role that greater justice can play in lessening pressures for war. Both can commit themselves to relieving injustices of all sorts as part of the work of peacemaking.

Furthermore pacifists and just-war advocates agree that education for peace calls for dissuading the public from slurring or demonizing the enemy people. They share a revulsion at racial, ethnic, or religious stereotyping or scapegoating. They both believe that when war occurs, education for peace entails teaching our children that it is a sorrowful, not a jubilant occasion, and that our enemies are not despicable evils, but fellow children of God.

Nevertheless pacifists and just-war advocates disagree in some ways about peacemaking. When pacifists speak of peacemaking, they often mean such actions as refusing to resort to war, refraining from military threats toward other countries, doing everything possible to negotiate an agreement short of war, and putting more money toward nonmilitary purposes and less toward armaments. Pacifists tend to interpret peacemaking as the opposite of military measures.

Just-war advocates usually work from a different understanding of how the world of international politics works. They believe that in the absence of military threats, some countries (like President Hussein's Iraq) will nevertheless initiate wars. Moreover, they argue that often one cannot bring an end to a war without threatening further attacks (as when the United States in 1953 sought to persuade China to agree to an end to the Korean War). From a just-war standpoint, Chamberlain's giving in to Hitler's demands at Munich was not an act of peacemaking, even though he thought it was at the time. From that standpoint, the lack of sufficient opposing military forces in the Middle East prior to August 2, 1990, and the absence of threats of retaliation if the Iraqis were to invade Kuwait were conditions encouraging war, not peace. From a just-war standpoint, then, there is no neat opposition between peacemaking and military measures. Peacemaking, from this standpoint, involves a mix of military and nonmilitary means, a mix of positive measures for justice and measures that restrain nations from unjustifiable wars.

If the world is one in which wars are likely to occur, Christians must concern themselves, not merely with condemning wars, but with exploring why wars occur. Simple problems have simple solutions, but war is not a simple problem. Pacifists and just-war advocates would do well to listen more to each other about the meaning of peacemaking. Each can learn from the other.

Education for peacemaking must be a high priority. It is something in which churches can continually be engaged. Yet we cannot educate well for peacemaking if our ideas of the causes and prevention of wars are inadequate. We shall not be educating for peace if we portray the world as it is not. The deep differences between crusaders, pacifists and just-war advocates are not only theological; they are also issues over what world politics is like. Working for peace requires attention to both.

NOTES

1. Is War a Crusade?

1. Quoted in Roland Bainton, *Christian Attitudes Toward War and Peace* (Nashville: Abingdon, 1960), p. 112.

2. James Turner Johnson, *Ideology, Reason, and the Limitation of War* (Princeton: Princeton University Press, 1975), p. 81.

3. Edward LeRoy Long, Jr., *War and Conscience in America* (Philadelphia: Westminster Press, 1968), p. 34.

4. David Irving, *The Destruction of Dresden* (New York: Ballantine Books, 1965).

5. Winston S. Churchill, *Closing the Ring* (Boston: Houghton Mifflin Co., 1951), p. 58.

6. Quoted in Robert E. Osgood, *Limited War* (Chicago: University of Chicago Press, 1957), pp. 35-36.

7. See ibid., pp. 3-4; and James Turner Johnson, *Just War Tradition and the Restraint of War* (Princeton: Princeton University Press, 1981), chap. viii.

2. The Pacifist Standpoint

1. See Bainton, *Christian Attitudes Toward War and Peace*, chapters 7, 10; and James F. Childress, "Pacifism," *The Westminster Dictionary of Christian Ethics* (Philadelphia: The Westminster Press, 1986), pp. 446-48.

2. Richard B. Gregg, *The Power of Nonviolence*, 2nd rev. ed. (New York: Schocken Books, 1966), pp. 36-41, 44, 46-47, 51, 93ff.

3. Yoder's witnessing argument is presented, among other places, in *The Politics of Jesus* (Grand Rapids: Eerdmans, 1972), esp. chapters 7 and 12.

4. Ibid., p. 158.

5. John Howard Yoder, *The Christian Witness to the State*, 3rd printing (Newton, Kansas: Faith and Life Press, 1977), pp. 9ff., 36-37, 55-56.

6. Hauerwas discusses war and violence especially in *The Peaceable Kingdom* (Notre Dame: University of Notre Dame Press, 1983) and *Against the Nations* (New York: Harper and Row, 1988).

7. *The Peaceable Kingdom*, p. 169, n. 19.

8. For an early statement of his view toward nonviolence, see Martin Luther King, Jr., *Stride Toward Freedom* (New York: Harper and Brothers, 1958), especially pp. 101-7, 213-22.

9. The most thorough study of nonviolent methods is Gene Sharp, *The Politics of Nonviolent Action* (Boston: Porter Sargent, 1973).

10. Reinhold Niebuhr, "Why the Christian Church Is Not Pacifist," *Christianity and Power Politics* (New York: Scribner's, 1940), pp. 1-32; see especially pp. 5-18.

11. Kenneth Waltz, *Man, the State, and War* (New York: Columbia University Press, 1965; first published, 1959).

12. William Robert Miller, in *Nonviolence: A Christian Interpretation* (London: George Allen & Unwin Ltd., 1964), is an example of one who avoids overstating the case for nonviolent means (p. 16).

13. Ramsey discusses the relation of love and violence in *Basic Christian Ethics* (New York: Scribner's, 1951), pp. 37-42; and *The Just War* (New York: Scribner's, 1968), pp. 142-43.

14. Yoder, *The Politics of Jesus*, p. 207n.

15. Niebuhr, *Christianity and Power Politics*, p. 5.

3. Just-War Thinking

1. The term "justifiable war" conveys the idea of morally right action concerning war. It suggests that the moral evils against which justifiable wars may be waged are matters of injustice, but it does not imply that the war involves no moral ambiguities or that justice is all on one side. The shorter term, "just war," is less cumbersome, though it may tempt us to overlook the reality of degrees of justice.

2. For a covenantal interpretation of Christian ethics, see my *Love and Conflict: A Covenantal Model of Christian Ethics* (Nashville: Abingdon, 1984).

3. This paragraph parallels the argument of Kenneth Waltz's *Man, the State, and War*.

4. Paul Ramsey, *The Just War*, pp. 142-43 (his italics).

5. Michael Walzer's *Just and Unjust Wars* (New York: Basic Books, 1977) is an insightful and influential discussion of the just-war criteria by a political philosopher.

6. James F. Childress, "Just-War Criteria," *Moral Responsibility in Conflicts* (Baton Rouge: Louisiana State University Press, 1982), pp. 75-76.

7. Cf. James Turner Johnson, *Ideology, Reason, and the Limitation of War*, pp. 40-41.

8. Cf. Childress, p. 80.

9. John C. Ford, S.J., "The Morality of Obliteration Bombing," *Theological Studies* 5 (#3, Sept. 1944):261-309.

10. Robert C. Batchelder, *The Irreversible Decision, 1939-1950* (Cambridge, Mass.: Houghton Mifflin, 1961).

11. Paul Ramsey, *War and the Christian Conscience* (Durham: Duke University Press, 1961); and *The Just War*.

4. What Can We Do?

1. Reuel L. Howe, *The Miracle of Dialogue* (New York: Seabury Press, 1963), p. 37.

2. See Nicholas Wolterstorff, *Until Justice and Peace Embrace* (Grand Rapids: Eerdmans, 1983), pp. 69-72.